WTF HAPPENED...

...no time to build a goat shed

by
CLAUDIA STAUBER

Cabin Talk Publishing
Morrisville, Vermont

1

This book is dedicated to the millions of
people who get fucked over by the
government every day.

We the people no longer believe in Democrats
vs. Republican, Black vs. White, Men Vs.
Women, Muslims vs. Christians and the lesser
of two evils.

This book is dedicated to the people who are
waking up to the fact that it is the
1% against the 99%!

Thank you!

Thank you Annie Malloy for keeping my grammar disasters to a minimum. All the mistakes that you guys will find are changes I made *after* Annie finished editing. Annie you have been a god send from the day I met you!

Thank you Arthur Robbins for making this beautiful cover and for not telling me to fuck off after the 100th change I wanted to have done. Most of all for being my friend and my family for life no matter how many times we hate each other!

Thank you Thomas Quay Williams aka William Wallace for traveling through the country with me and promoting sanity in this time of utter chaos. For being a crusader and for speaking the truth when that is a very rare commodity!

Thank you to all the people who watch Cabin Talk and who encourage me on a daily basis to open my mouth against injustice and lies. All of you mean so very much to me and my path in life.

There are no words that could ever express how grateful I am for your comments, your likes and your hearts on my screen!

Disclaimer:

First off I want to let you all know that this book is my opinion, not fact. It is based on reading and collecting information from sources I know and trust and from my own observations. This book is biased and no I am not trying to be a credible journalist (there are only a few left anyway), nor am I trying to convince anybody of anything. I am simply extremely pissed off and I am trying to share my two cents with you guys on the state of this country and our world, as I know it!

CONTENT

WTF Happened to Elections especially in 2016?

Now there is a subject that I don't even know where to start! The Democratic primaries were a joke plain and simple. They were a disgrace to democracy. They were rigged! Why did I even follow them you might ask? Well, senator Bernie Sanders is my senator since I live in Vermont and I have adored the man since the first time I heard about him years ago, actually he was one of the reasons I moved to Vermont. I thought a state that has a senator like Bernie has got to be a great place.
So Bernie runs for office of president of the United States and loses to Hillary Clinton.

HOW CAN THAT BE?

Just another Bernie rally

Nobody knew Bernie when he started, well only about 2% had ever heard his name. But like an absolute wildfire his rallies grew from hundreds of people to thousands of people to tens of thousands of people. Hillary on the other hand couldn't fill a ladies bathroom on a Saturday night in a busy bar if she tried. Well the occasional high school gymnasium filled halfway up but that was the best she could do. Hundreds of thousands of people started promoting Bernie, from memes, to videos, to online talk shows and millions of individuals started to donate and we all know what that amount averaged out to be. **$27!!!**

The revolution started becoming reality. A revolution Bernie was talking about in every speech and he always emphasized that he cannot do it alone. *Only if all of us pull together can we win against the oligarchy!* There was an energy and an enthusiasm that had never been experienced before by my generation or younger *ever!* The voting started and voter turnout was through the roof, in almost every single state; people stood in line for hours wanting to cast their votes.

BUT HE LOST? WTF?

There is a machine at work, a well-oiled machine of corruption called the DNC and they pulled every dirty trick in the book to rig the elections in Hillary's favor. From voter suppression, to rigged voting machines, to throwing out hundreds of thousands of voters like in New York, closing polling places, to Bill Fucking Clinton going inside voting places and holding people up for hours like in Massachusetts and in Illinois. California took the cake with provisional ballots that got handed out like candy on Halloween. And yet nobody up high complained, including Bernie!

What the fuck?

The states where the rigging was hard to do because of paper ballots, Bernie generally won. The states with voting machines produced by a company that has been a Hillary supporter, were the absolute worst places and Bernie lost in those. President Obama remained silent, Hillary Clinton remained silent and Bernie Sanders remain silent. Bernie supporters went crazy and couldn't understand the world anymore, Hillary Clinton supporters were saying that Bernie Sanders supporters are paranoid and joining the right-wing crazy train and the media remained completely silent.

Fast forward to the DNC convention in July 2016. What a cluster fuck!

The DNC convention before the start

I had no idea that a first world country could be so corrupt under the very eyes of its citizens. I think it is safe to say that we no longer live in even the faintest hint of a democracy. How could we have all missed it when it was stolen? How could we not have listened to the people that told us that it was being stolen, people like Chris Hedges and even George Carlin knew it. I guess we are comfortable enough still that we disregard all the signs. But if you would have been at the DNC shit show, which is what I call that rigged bullshit of a convention, you would have seen it with your very own eyes and you would have been also completely awakened.

It started with WikiLeaks releasing emails that *proved* that the DNC rigged the elections in Hillary's favor. It was indisputable proof, proof to the point where Debbie Wasserman Schultz had to resign as the head of the DNC. You cannot imagine the cheering, the noise level that happened when it was announced that Debbie Wasserman Schultz resigned. What happened next only an hour or so later is going to blow your mind if you haven't heard it already. Hillary HIRED HER and the reasoning she said she wanted her, is for her CONTINUED SUPPORT OF HER CAMPAIGN!!!

NO FUCKING WORDS!!!

Thousands of people protesting in the streets of Philly

It went downhill from there although you wouldn't think that's even fucking possible. Bernie volunteers got kicked out of the convention and were replaced with Hillary volunteers, Bernie delegates did a massive walk out and demonstrations with sit-ins outside in the media tent, but almost no reporting on that. On the last day when Hillary was giving her speech the seats of the delegates who were supporting Bernie were replaced with actors so it showed "UNITY" which of course didn't exist. They were protesting the loss of our democracy! Bernie signs that they had in their hands were taken away from them and ripped up. Is this what democracy looks like?

some of the delegates, THIS is what democracy looks like!

A friend of mine actually smuggled some Jill Stein signs into the convention and they held them up as they were putting up the big Hillary banner. Our beautiful delegates were so creative in a time when they were being silenced! Dissent had to take on a whole new form.

It is heartbreaking to see democracy disappear and it will take all of us to get it back! *It will take people from the left as well as from the right because all of us at this point are in the same boat.* We might not agree on details but the truth is that democracy has been stolen from all of us and the owners of this country and soon the world are now ruling us, if we don't stand up *now*.

WTF Happened to Bernie?

That has got to be the million-dollar question. This wonderful old man decides with his wife Jane that he will have to run for president because nobody else is willing to stand up to the oligarchy.

I was in Burlington when he announced that he would run for president in front of 5000 people. You can't imagine the noise level when he said those words. People were cheering to the point where we had no voice left and we all were crying, tears of hope, tears of love, tears for each other and mostly for Bernie out of gratitude. It was a special day and I will never forget it. That was the first rally Bernie had and it was one of many. He really caught on fire and the saying "feel the bern" was absolutely perfect.

Every single person who met him fell in love with him. We fell in love with his integrity, his wisdom, his message, but most of all with his humility and humanity. Bernie was one of us and he didn't change into somebody else as time went on. Just the contrary, he became more one of us if that was even possible. His honesty, his candidness and his bluntness are what we all came to admire. Millennials were as crazy about him as they would have been about any rock star. But grandmothers and grandfathers were equally taken by him and his message. People stood in line for a few hours, which was not unusual of a wait to get in.

Bernie's announcement rally at the waterfront in Burlington VT

The elections started to happen and Bernie won some. The ones that he lost started to be suspicious. Polling places were closed, people were dropped from voting lists, and states with machines that could easily be tampered with he lost the most yet the states with paper ballots he usually won.

Bernie stayed on message. He ran a clean campaign and did not attack Hillary Clinton on personal issues, which would have been incredibly easy. Instead he kept pushing the issues that were important to normal people. He was lobbying for $15 minimum wage, equal pay, tuition free state colleges and universities, universal healthcare, stop the TPP, and many more.

Bernie delegates made signs for truth out of Hillary signs!

I don't know why he never called out the election fraud that was so blatant it was painful to watch. He never complained even when illegal things happened in plain sight like Bill Clinton holding up the voting in Massachusetts for a total of eight hours. Lawsuits were filed but Bernie remained silent. He always however said that he would take it all the way to Philadelphia and contest the convention.

About four weeks before the convention Bernie had a meeting with President Obama at the White House. He came out and had a press conference and he was visibly pissed off but he still said we will wait till every vote is counted and we will take it to Philadelphia. An hour later President Obama endorsed Hillary Clinton which is completely unprecedented that a sitting president endorses a candidate before the convention. The next day Elizabeth Warren who we always thought carried exactly Bernie's message and was very progressive, also endorsed Hillary Clinton.

Bernie people immediately turned on Elizabeth Warren and I honestly believe she was holding out till the end so she could become the vice president of whoever would get the nomination. Well she got totally fucked over and it serves her right. She could have supported Bernie from the beginning and it would have made a big difference but instead she played the political game and lost everything.

Only about a week before the convention Bernie and Hillary held an event in New Hampshire where he announced that he would endorse Hillary Clinton. I was there and I cannot describe the heartache we all felt. I held back my tears until I was out of the building, which I left immediately after Bernie's speech because I couldn't bear hearing Hillary boast. She had stolen the election and now Bernie was standing behind her.

This picture says it all...

Seeing Bernie up on stage I could feel his pain as

tangibly as my own and writing this right now I have tears in my eyes again. People started calling him a sellout and a traitor but watching him saying those words my heart was breaking for him more than for myself.

The problem is we all fell in love, literally! We fell in love with this old man; we fell in love so deeply that letting go is very hard to do. Men and women fell in love with him and how could we not. He brought us all back to a place of love instead of hatred. He evoked this feeling in us that we are all the same and we are all in this together. This feeling of love, non-judgment, and acceptance of each other which in turn allowed us to accept ourselves.

BUT the good news is we can continue, we can continue on the same path of accepting each other and ourselves. To spread kindness and love and to stand up for what is right!

How could we ever forget when the bird landed on Bernie's podium!

WTF is Black Lives Matter?

We hear all this talk about black lives matter versus all lives matter. What is that all about? Well it is very simple, the reason why it's called black lives matter is because in this country black lives do not matter as much as white lives and that is simply a fact. Racism is alive and well in many parts of this country and if you needed any proof then Donald Trump is it. He caters to racism and bigotry, and people are flocking to him. Granted, the people are uneducated and ignorant but still there are many of them.

BLACK LIVES
MATTER

I talked to a group of young black men in Houston and they were beautiful and educated young guys and they were discussing how black people are treated very differently at the University campus. I had a wonderful conversation with them and I couldn't agree more that there is still a two-class system in this country.

Trying to simply ignore the problem of racism will not do anything to heal it. It will simply put a bigger divide into this country since black people feel they are not being heard and white people pretend that it's not happening.

Now here is a test, ask any white person if they would rather be black and I guarantee you that everybody will rather stay white, which proves that there is racism.

In a time of unprecedented police brutality against black people we need to wake up and open our eyes.

How many white people get killed by black cops?

How many black people get killed by white cops?

I made my point! We can no longer sit here and pretend that everything is OK we need to actively work on bringing people together no matter what the color. Most of all we need to stand up against the injustice that is happening to black communities. It is our duty if we are white to stand up for black people. Just like it is the duty of Hillary supporters to stand up against the election fraud. If my candidate would have done what Hillary's team has done during the elections I would be calling it out and I would no longer stand behind that candidate.

If we are quiet in the face of injustice we are as guilty as the people that are committing the crime!

Hitler did not become so powerful because so many people supported him; he became so powerful because so few people spoke out against him.

The number of pigments in our skin should not be the judge what kind of a person we stand across from. It should be the integrity, the character, the kindness, the honesty and the values of the person that we are looking at. Dr. Martin Luther King made important leaps in that movement however we really have a long way to go and ignoring it will not solve it.

We need to have communities that are of all colors and walk towards people of different races instead of away from them. We have to embrace our differences instead of hating them.

So when we say #BlackLivesMatter we really have to stand behind those words and only when black lives matter as much as white lives can we say #AllLivesMatter but we have a long ways to go until that can actually be a hash tag we are allowed to use.

WTF Happened to Our Prison System?

When under Bill Clinton most prisons became private corporations instead of government institutions, profits became more important than the innocence of people. The privatization of prisons opened the door to complete corruption of the system. People are getting locked up for nonviolent crimes for many years, Marijuana possession being one of them. Of course there are crimes that people commit that should be punished with a prison sentence however most of the people in prison nowadays are people that have not committed a violent crime and yet they are rotting away for years.

Why is that important to have so many people in prison you might ask?

Well the short answer is that it is free labor for big corporations. Prisons are now the new sweatshops of this country. They get paid basically nothing, the government pays for room and board and corporations get things manufactured in prisons that they can then sell for enormous profits. Hey it's a great deal just not for the people having to sit in prison cells, but who the hell cares about them they are just human beings and disposable and mostly not white so that's a double 'who gives a shit'!

Prisons are the new slave labor camps of the 21st century. They are a way for corporate America to increase profits and cut cost.

We have to stop the school to prison pipeline with kids

barely out of school and they are already in prisons. They don't know any different and they give up on life before it has ever begun. We need to improve schools in poor neighborhoods and we have a moral obligation to invest in their future with education instead of incarceration!

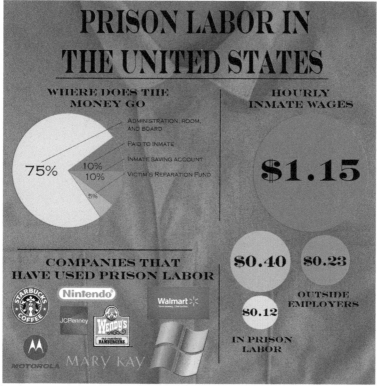

Look at some of the companies that are profiting of prisons!

We have to build schools instead of prisons, we have to invest in the education and future of our children, and we have to create opportunities for them so they can start a life worth living.

Recently Baltimore could not afford to fix up their

25

schools for 10 million dollars but gave 30 million to the prison complex for juveniles! Now there is something so very wrong about that and it has to change. We need to stand up and hold PUBLIC OFFICIALS (yes they are supposed to represent us the people) accountable or make them resign!

We need people in office that are not bought by the prison industrial complex and our number one goal has to be to get money out of politics! As long as corporations can buy public officials nothing will change. They will be beholden to their benefactors and not to us.

We have to overturn Citizens United!

WTF is Citizens United?

Well, Citizens United is anything but that. It does not unite citizens it creates the opposite it gives corporations the power to buy themselves elections.

Citizens United was founded in 1988 by basically the Koch brothers, David and Charles Koch, two multi gazillionares who would love to get rid of anything that is good for normal and underprivileged people. If they would have their way they would eradicate Social Security, healthcare for all, minimum wage, and any kind of welfare.

The Supreme Court eventually decided in 2009 that corporations are people and that super PACs can be formed and pour unlimited amounts of money into elections. What it comes down to is that now millionaires and billionaires can give candidates as much money as they want and of course needless to say they will only do that in return for passing laws that they want in order to make more money.

We no longer have elections we now have corporate mouthpieces sitting in Congress and the Senate and other elected offices. They are no longer for the most part representatives of the people but they are representatives of the corporations and Citizens United was the big starting point of that. They just did not have the blessing of the Supreme Court until fairly recently.

Now don't get discouraged because we did see in the Bernie campaign that a candidate can run an amazing election, being funded only by the people. We also need to ensure that we elect people into office that want to keep money out of the elections.

If a corporation funds somebody, you already know that they will not have your back, but that they will have the backs of the corporations.

It is vitally important that you are vetting the people you are intending to vote for whether that is on a town, state, or federal level. You need to ask them hard questions and look at their platform.

Nothing is more dangerous to the establishment then an informed electorate!!!

We do have the power to overturn Citizens United. There are petitions that we need to get behind and we have to carefully select new people that are running for public offices who actually have OUR interests in mind instead of the interest of the oligarchy. Finding people with integrity who actually want to serve the people will be up to us and we have to be the ones running for those offices.

"We are the ones we have been waiting for!!!"
- Jill Stein -

TPP
EXPLAINED

Corporations want a law to make it against the law to make a law against them.

memaginatior

The TPP is the most dangerous treaty of our time for the US and the rest of the world!

This is definitely one of our biggest issues if not the biggest one! The TPP short for Trans Pacific Partnership is being sold as a trade agreement however less than a quarter is actually about trade, the rest is a corporate takeover of this world.

There are actually three different agreements that corporate America has been working on with over 600 of their lawyers for the last few years. They are called TPP, TTIP and TiSA and are more or less the same thing just geared towards different areas of the planet. It used to be kept and written in complete secrecy but thanks to WikiLeaks it became more public. Now, what the fuck needs to be kept so secret that nobody knows anything about when it affects the whole world. Think about that for a moment!!!

It will affect all areas of our lives, from the Internet to healthcare, from the environment to jobs. It will affect normal people extremely badly; however, it'll be the cats meow for corporations and to say it in the words of Hillary Clinton "it is the gold standard of trade agreements".

Delegates protesting the TPP at the DNC

There will be an estimated loss of about 450,000 jobs in the US alone that will be outsourced to other countries for low wages. Workers rights will be gone if they hurt the profits of multinational corporations. Laws we now have to protect the environment and workers rights will be super ceded by protecting corporate profits and even PROJECTED profits!!!

People will have less access to prescription drugs because there will be a rise in prices as well as a delayed time for getting generic prescriptions on the market. Pharmaceutical companies will have higher profits than they already do now. This is such an important point because people's lives are really on the line since not being able to get the drugs they need will mean a death sentence to some of them. If you think you struggle with paying for your prescription drugs now, wait until the TPP has been signed!

The Trans Pacific Partnership (TPP)

A short explanation of the TPP on different issues

Here is the scariest part: you can forget about the laws of this country, even the Supreme Court. Because corporations will have the right to hold secret tribunals and decide in those how much money countries have to pay them if the laws they have, are against their profits. What does that mean in simple language? Well, let's say there is a law against fracking in several states but the corporations that are fracking and the oil industry feel that this will be against their profits, then they have the right to overturn those environmental laws and sue different states or the whole country for lost *projected profits* for millions if not billions of dollars.

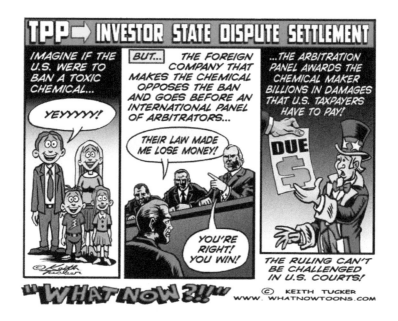

What The Fuck???

Our Internet freedom will also be finally taken away in the form of copyright laws. They have tried it a few times in the past but never succeeded, because people would stand up against those kinds of laws! It is somewhat complicated but they will finally be able to control our Internet. The punishment of breaking those "laws" will no longer be about fines, it will be about going to jail.

And last but not least the TPP does not have an exit clause or an expiration date which means once it is signed into law it will be there FOREVER!!! That is absolutely unprecedented in the history of any treaty that has ever been signed!!!

So all in all the TPP has no advantages at all for this

country or other countries. It is basically a mass enslavement of workers and the middle class. President Obama is trying to push it through on fast track before he's out of office. He's lobbying hard for it and he's basically telling people things that are untrue about the TPP. He, just like most of our politicians is beholden to corporate America and therefore only trying to push their agenda instead of your and my interest. They are spouting off things like because we are living in a global economy, that we need agreements globally but what they fail to tell you is that it will be devastating to the American workers. It is NAFTA on steroids and we all know that NAFTA basically destroyed the middle class and good paying jobs by outsourcing most of them to other countries.

In the last 15 years we have lost 60,000 factories! Those are not 60,000 jobs, those are 60,000 FACTORIES!!!

So please say STOP the TPP!!!

People are protesting the TPP around the world!

WTF Happened to Our Schools?

When standardized tests were introduced in American schools, it was the beginning of the end of learning. No Child left behind, are you fucking kidding me! The thing that corporate America does so well is taking a narrative and making it the opposite of what it actually is! When the Bush administration introduced no Child left behind, it was the end of education and critical thinking and the beginning of turning kids into drones. Learning is actually no longer the main prerogative, what has become the main goal is to have a homogenous group of people by the time they leave school.

The arts have been all but eradicated in the curriculum. How can that even be! The brain needs to be stimulated in different ways in order to function at its best capacity. Creativity is imperative for anybody to learn on different levels. Kids whose creativity is encouraged learn faster and easier and with more joy which cannot be emphasized enough.

Children in this day and age are trained from the age of zero that they have to produce and succeed. For Christ sake there are videos for infants so they get already programmed and to ensure that they will eventually get into the right preschool, which in turn gets them into the right elementary school, which in turn gets them into the right middle school, which in turn gets them into the right high school, which in turn gets them into the right college, which in turn gets them into the right company, which in turn makes them into higher paid slave jobs!

Where in this whole bullshit does happiness factor in?

When is there a time in a child's life nowadays for them to actually be children? When is there time for them to just be outside and explore the world? They are in school for too many hours, and then come home and do homework for another couple hours and then they have other commitments. Their mind does not run free and simply relax.

They have to run from soccer practice, to baseball, to football, to hockey, or best-case scenario to learning the piano, and ballet lessons. When do kids have time to literally do nothing or just play in the dirt? Kids are being disconnected from this beautiful nature that we have at an early age. They no longer know how to grow food, what plants really look like and what they are for and how animals should be treated. They no longer learn basic cooking skills or how to make anything, shop skills have completely been eradicated because if you can fix something or make something then you will not buy it from corporations that make their shit in China for pennies and then sell it to you for dollars!

Also when did the schoolbooks become corporate advertising tools? How can there be even the word Coca-Cola in a schoolbook? When I was at the University of Houston recently I was in shock what they have to offer the kids that go to school there in food choices. That was McDonald's, sbarro pizza, some chain Chinese place who's name I forgot and a pseudo health food offering chain that offered shakes and some devoid of nutrient salads. However the health food place was closed most of the time!

Our kids are under-nourished and overfed and everybody knows that the brain cannot work correctly if it doesn't have the right nutrients to feed the neurons in the brain. The children of this world are the future and I was beyond thrilled to see that so many young people got involved in the Bernie Sanders campaign. You guys are the ones who have to take back our planet from the corporations and the oligarchy!

I am sorry we leave you with such a rotten deal but the students have always been the ones to be in the streets and to fight for their rights and in this case and in this time it will have to be a formidable fight for you guys to still have a planet to live on!

WTF Happened to Our Media?

The media used to be a place where people could get a mostly unbiased recount of facts; a place where you could get information and then form an educated opinion. Well that has gone so far down the tubes that we will probably never see that again on TV. 6 corporations now own over 90% of the media. You can pretty much turn on any TV station that is a so-called news station and you will hear the almost identical narrative. Yes Fox will spin it a little more to the right and MSNBC will try to make it sound a little bit more to the left but the message will be identical. And any journalist who actually tries to report the news will be fired. There are people who are trying to report what is actually going on however they will not be long in this world of corporate propaganda.

Media Consolidation:

THE ILLUSION OF CHOICE

Media has never been more consolidated. 6 media giants now control a staggering 90% of what we read, watch, or listen to.

THESE SIX COMPANIES ARE:

GE	NEWS-CORP	DISNEY	VIACOM	TIME WARNER	CBS
Notable Properties:	Notable Properties:	Notable Properties:	Notable Properties:	Notable Properties:	Notable Properties:
COMCAST	FOX	ABC	MTV	CNN	SHOWTIME
NBC	WALL STREET JOURNAL	ESPN	NICK JR	HBO	SMITHSONIAN CHANNEL
UNIVERSAL PICTURES	NEW YORK POST	PIXAR	BET	TIME	NFL.COM
FOCUS FEATURES		MIRAMAX	CMT	WARNER BROS	JEOPARDY
		MARVEL STUDIOS	PARAMOUNT PICTURES		60 MINUTES

Also have you noticed that most people who are now reporting the "news" look the same? All the women are beautiful and all the men look like Ken from Barbie. They all have perfect hair, perfect teeth, and perfect bodies. They are what we should strive for and are just another advertising billboard. They carry the subliminal message of corporate America that you need to look perfect on the outside and with all the shit we're selling you, we can help you with that! If you are not perfect you better not be on TV.

The corporate media refused to report on the unbelievable election fraud, which should have been the number one story for months and would have been eradicated if they had reported it. The corporate media should every single day, report on events that are detrimental to our planet. From Fukushima, to the BP oil spill, which both still have horrendous ramifications to our icebergs which are melting at a much more rapid pace than any scientist would have ever anticipated, to the dying of our forests and the acidification of our oceans. We have record heat every year and our planet is dying!

But not a word in mainstream media!

Instead we hear on the NEWS about people like Kim Kardashian and I can't even tell you how much that fucking agitates me!!!

The media is one of the main ways for corporate America to get their way. They will "report" at nausea on a subject that they want to see done. For example they would constantly ask Bernie when he will drop out and they did that during a time when he was in spite of the rigging, was winning in sometimes multiple states in a row! Remember when they wanted to push the Iraq war? The only word you would hear on TV was *terrorist!*

Also have you noticed what the corporate media is doing? Instead of reporting on the actual story like for instance that Hillary Clinton had a private email server and national top secret files got out in the open, they are reporting on whether it was the Russians that leaked the story. Who gives a flying fuck who leaked the story, the important part is the STORY!!!

○ WHO OWNS THE BIG TV NETWORKS?

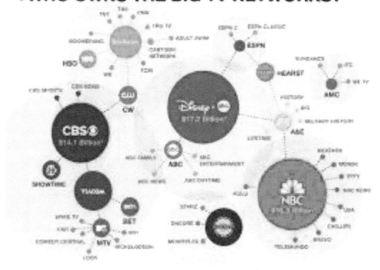

When the facts were in that Debbie Wasserman Schultz rigged the elections, and I mean national elections for the presidency of the United States were officially RIGGED, they instead made the story about apologizing to Bernie Sanders that they made religion an issue when they were discussing how exactly they were rigging the election.

THE FUCKING ELECTIONS IN THIS COUNTRY WERE STOLEN!!!

THAT should have been the headline news every single fucking day. If you are smart you cancel your TV today and instead take that money and invest it into the future of your children by buying them books and taking them on trips into nature.

Some of my favorite news people and citizen journalists.

As to the news, go online and find credible news sources like Democracy Now and get your news from people like Chris Hedges who is truly still a journalist with integrity. But be aware and be on your toes because even so called independent news sources get bought up by the mainstream media once they get popular and become just another mouthpiece for corporate America. That is what happened in my eyes with The Young Turks who were fabulous. But when the horrendous election fraud happened in the California democratic primaries they were completely silent and started to pound the Hillary pavement. That's when I learned that they had sold out. It's a shame because I really liked watching them but c'est la vie we move on!

Pay attention to citizen journalists like Steve Grumbine with Real Progressives, Debbie the Sane Progressive, Tim Black, Ed Higgins, Lee Camp with Redacted Tonight and Niko House to name a few. And of course last but not least Cabin Talk, which I started out of total frustration during the primaries.

So please disconnect your cable and don't buy into the brain washing of the establishment. Remember smart people are so much harder to fool!

WTF Happened to Health Care?

In the richest country in the history of the world, healthcare should be a right for all its citizens. People should not lose their home if they get sick. Nobody who gets cancer or has a heart attack should have to choose between their home or getting treatment. Parents who have a sick child or a child with a devastating illness are being held hostage by the healthcare system. When a child can be saved yet it is too expensive for the parents, what kind of a decision is that to make for a human being? It should not have to be a decision that needs to be made in the first place, it should be taken care of by healthcare for everybody.

The pharmaceutical industry is one of the richest and most profitable industries in the world. Prescription drug prices are through the roof in this country. Sometimes more than 100 fold compared to other countries. You might ask why that is the case. The pharmaceutical industry has an army of lobbyists that are hanging out at state houses and in Washington around the clock. The purpose is simply to pass laws that are advantageous to the pharmaceutical industry. There is actually a law that prohibits Medicaid from negotiating drug prices. And that we are paying the highest drug prices in the world, I'm sure has nothing to do with the fact that big Pharma has roughly 2500 lobbyists running around.

Some people might tell you that the US has the best doctors in the best hospitals and the best medications but that is not true. Other countries also have phenomenal doctors and an extraordinary healthcare system and yet nobody has to pay out-of-pocket. Do those countries have higher taxes? Yes maybe slightly but not by much. The payout however of such a system is so magnificent because of all the benefits that it would bring for each family, and most of all the peace of mind that people would get by knowing they are taken care of in case they get sick.

Imagine you can go to any doctor when you get sick

and get treatment. If you need a drugs you go to the pharmacy and pick them up at no cost to you. A lot of times those countries also pay for preventative care like massage or chiropractic treatment. Dental care is also included. In short a first world country should take care of its citizens. We are the ones paying the taxes so we should benefit from them as well. Of course healing people is not the goal of big Pharma and the healthcare system.

There is no money in healthy people and there is no money in dead people. The money is right in the middle, sick enough to need a continuous flow of meds but not dead yet.

TRUE HEALTHCARE REFORM STARTS IN YOUR KITCHEN, NOT IN WASHINGTON.
FB.COM/GROWFOODNOTLAWNS

Now of course we could put big Pharma out of business simply by making better life choices. You see it all ties together. If we would eat healthy organic food then the estimates are that about 80% of all health issues could be eradicated. I pray for the day when we all collectively wake up and tell those corporations to go screw themselves by growing our own food, by bartering with our neighbors and by no longer buying into this absolutely corrupt system.

WTF is Fracking?

Well first of all it's a nightmare for this planet. Fracking basically drills very deep holes into our earth, inject chemicals and in turn gets out natural gas and oil.

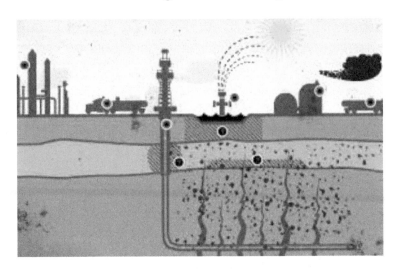

Doesn't sound too bad, does it? Well there's a big problem with that. The chemicals that are injected seep into the ground water and contaminate the water supplies of the whole area and sometimes far beyond since the underground aquifers are like underground rivers and move all over the place. You might have seen pictures or videos of places that have fracking and now people's water that is coming out of their faucets is no longer clear and some of it can actually be lit up with a match and starts to burn. And that is what people are supposed to still drink and that is also what the corporations that are fracking are telling them is completely safe!

Nothing like some nice clean burning water

One of the side effects of fracking is that it leaks enormous amounts of methane into the air and methane is 86 times more detrimental to our planet than carbon dioxide. This is not my number, this is the number given by the EPA in 2015. Now we all know that the CO_2 emissions are already too high to sustain the planet and we can see that because the planet is heating up more every year. Again July 2016 was the hottest one on record and the year before that was the hottest and the year before that was the hottest and so on and so forth. A new record is being broken every single year and if you haven't noticed yet we are burning up!!!

HYDRAULIC FRACTURING & WATER

Natural gas plays a key role in our nation's clean energy future. The U.S. has vast reserves of natural gas that are commercially viable as a result of advances in horizontal drilling and hydraulic fracturing technologies enabling greater access to gas in shale formations. Responsible development of America's shale gas resources offers important economic, energy security, and environmental benefits.

-EPA

by h2odistributors.com

Primary U.S. Energy Use
(By Fuel Type, 2011)

- Renewables (including biofuels)
- Liquid Biofuels
- Natural Gas
- Nuclear
- Coal
- Petroleum & Liquids

Natural Gas accounts for 25% of all the energy used in the U.S.

By 2035 it is estimated that **46%** of all natural gas will come from **Fracking**

The average fracking well **requires around 5,000,000 gallons of water** to operate over its lifetime

That's about **167** tanker cars full* *30,000 gal sized

Water is combined **with sand and a cocktail of chemicals to help in the fracking process** and then injected into the well

90% Water
9.5% Sand
0.5% Chemical Additives

Around 750 compounds are listed in a 2011 report to Congress, ranging from additives found in food and common houshold cleaners to known carcinogens.

20%-40% of this fluid flows back to the surface, polluted with dissolved solids **toxic chemicals & slightly irradiated.**

If drilled too shallow or not inspected properly **wells can leak natural gas** into the air and **water**

The process also causes measurable **but small earthquakes** (1-4 on the Richter scale)

© h2odistributors.com

There is another little side effect that fracking has which is earthquakes. In Oklahoma for example the amount of earthquakes was very small, a few each year basically summed it up, until 2010 when they started fracking and it jumped to over 1000 earthquakes a year! By 2015 the number of earthquakes was over 2500 a year!!! Do you think it could have anything to do with the fact that they started fracking in 2010?

Of course they will try to sell you on the idea of fracking by saying that it is number one completely safe, number two you can make some money by letting them frack on your land or the states land and it will create an increase in revenue, number three it will make us less dependent on foreign oil. What all of that is, is utter bullshit! It is anything but safe! There isn't enough money we can pay for no longer having clean water! And if we no longer want to be dependent on foreign oil then we need to immediately invest in alternative energies that are safe to our planet. We have wind, we have solar and many other options and we have brilliant people that are dying to get grants to explore alternative energies on a much broader level. Yet most of the government subsidies are still going to big oil even though they have record earnings every quarter.

I think it is high time that we call bullshit on it and if they are trying to frack in your state please join or create an initiative against it. We have the numbers to shut down any operation that destroys our planet and creates an environment that will no longer sustain our children and grandchildren!

Please get on board NOW!!!

Our power is truly in the numbers and we can stop the destruction of our mother earth!

WTF where is the Alternative Energy?

Alternative energy in this country is slow to blossom. Why? The answer is pretty simple! There is still way too much money to be made in oil! The oil companies have no interest in alternative energies because the less oil eventually there will be, the more they will be able to raise the prices and make money. We have amazing alternatives to oil already and yet they are not getting the traction they need and deserve.

Slowly, very slowly we are starting to see solar farms and solar panels on roofs but it is still fairly expensive for people to put them on their homes. We have wind farms but again we could have many more of them and we could have them on a smaller scale at private homes if they would be more subsidized by the government. If your plot of land works for wind then why not have a small windmill?

President Jimmy Carter is my hero in more ways then one. When he became president he installed solar panels on the White House and think about it, that was decades ago. If he could have remained in office longer, what a change that could have made to this country and our environment. Sadly Ronald Reagan got elected next and one of the first things he did is take the solar panels off the White House roof.

What the fuck WHY???

The answer is fairly simple, Reagan got money from big oil and the last thing they wanted to promote is solar energy.

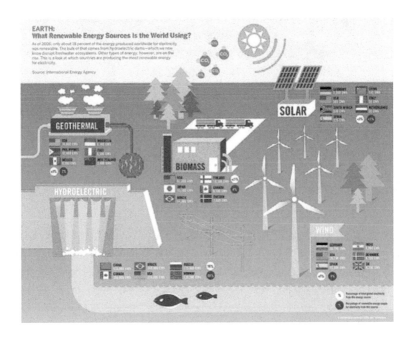

Clean renewable energies will be the lifeblood for the next generations and are mandatory if we want to hand down a livable planet to the kids of this world. We don't have all the time in the world; we have a small window of opportunity to save our precious planet.

We have to make better choices individually but also our government has to promote clean energy *now.*

When you enter the voting booth, you have to be educated about who promotes clean alternative energy sources and who was lobbied by Big Oil. We need to become very informed citizens so they can no longer make decisions based on money but on what their constituents actually want.

WTF is WikiLeaks?

WikiLeaks is an international non-profit journalistic organization that publishes secret information, news leaks, and classified media from anonymous sources (according to Wikipedia)

Julian Assange is the founder of WikiLeaks and started the organization in 2006. He is an acclaimed Journalist and a real truth teller. He is also dangerous to the establishment and therefore in grave danger.

Whistle blowers also known as heroes!

There are accusations against him for sexual assault in Sweden and because of that he has been in the embassy of Ecuador in England since 2012 to escape prosecution (however I don't believe for a second the rape allegations). He can not leave the embassy because he would be immediately captured by the authorities in England and in my opinion he would be handed over to the US and would never see the light of day again.

Over the years he has seriously shaken up the establishment and has brought real truth to light. The most recent leaks were in connection with the DNC. The emails he released were showing clearly that the primary elections on the democratic side where rigged in Hillary Clinton's favor against Bernie Sanders. The proof was so undeniable that Debbie Wasserman Schultz had to resign as the head of the DNC! But no problem for Debbie because Hillary *hired* her a couple hours later to "continue the support for her campaign"!!!

Another serious WTF moment in my life!

On top of it Debbie is still running for a seat in the House in Florida. How the hell can somebody who admitted that she committed a crime (last time I checked it was still against the law to rig the elections) run for one of the highest offices in the country?

Anyway, back to WikiLeaks and Julian Assange. They are now labeling him as a cyber terrorist and the US is trying to pressure the Ecuadorian government to extradite him. The way they are doing it is by basically trying to bully them via the media and the narrative that it would be disadvantageous to Ecuador economically to give asylum to a cyber terrorist.

I pray every day that they will not do that and instead keep him save. We all have to sign petitions for his release and safety because whistle blowers should be revered and not be looked at as criminals. Edward Snowden and Chelsea Manning are also seen as criminals instead of the heroes that they are!!!

"In a time of deceit, telling the truth is a revolutionary act!" George Orwell

WTF Happened, why all those Wars!

War is money and I could actually end the chapter right here.

It is absolutely criminal to invade other countries for no reason at all and take their resources. It is modern day colonialism. The Iraq war is the absolute perfect example. We had no business going into that country at all instead we should have minded our own business. But they had stuff we wanted! So a narrative was created that was perpetually saying terrorist, terrorist, terrorist, terrorist, terror! Saddam Hussein was portrayed as the man who had weapons of mass destruction and also of hiding terrorists.

But people weren't OK with just invading another country we needed to have a reason. So 9/11 happened and all I'm gonna say about that is that there is a petition of over 2000 engineers, structural engineers worldwide, to have an independent investigation! After 9/11 people were OK with finding the terrorists who did it. If it meant invading other countries so be it.

And there you go, we are going into Iraq!

George W. Bush and Dick Cheney were all too eager to get troops on the ground and to bomb the shit out of this country that had done nothing wrong or against us. They had no weapons of mass destruction and they were not hiding any terrorists. However Halliburton who Dick Cheney of course was on the board of, made a fortune during the war. They got most of the contracts and they were all too eager to work on the destruction of that country and the so-called rebuilding of it. The weapons industry was profoundly happy. More weapons could be sold to all sides and of course we need to arm all sides so there is actually conflict. This is what the US has been doing in all of the countries that we have invaded.

By the way under Secretary Clinton more weapon sales were approved then under any other Secretary of State.

By taking out a dictator we leave a void and it is getting filled by extremists. Whether we are talking about Al Qaeda or ISIS doesn't really matter, the outcome is the same except that with every regime change war we are creating more enemies and depleting our human resources.

Imagine if that would be your child!

Are you really surprised that people hate us? Frankly I am surprised that they don't hate us more! We drone bomb other countries indiscriminately. Private citizens get killed and when you see the dead children of those countries lying in the dirt and mothers and fathers crying over their babies, how can they not become enemies of the US?

I need to tell you guys about something else and that is called depleted uranium, which has been used on bombs in Iraq. They are basically small dirty bombs and what that has done to the Iraqi children is almost unspeakable. Parents no longer ask whether the child is a boy or a girl, they simply ask whether it is healthy because so many are born with horrific deformities. As I'm typing this I am crying because my heart is so sad for the people of Iraq.

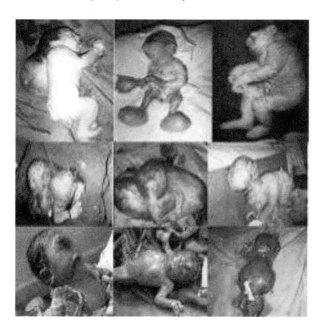

The cost of war is so very much higher than we think it is. I watch soldiers come home not only sick in their bodies but sick in their minds from the horrific things they have seen. They get a really rotten deal and our veterans are not taken care of by our government. They are used and are seen as disposable!

By the way, did you notice that now they signed a law that women could also be drafted? I just wanted to bring that to your attention because unless they would be revving up for more wars why would that even be necessary!

This is what to cost of war looks like!

If we do not elect public officials from the presidency down, we will have more wars and more enemies on our hands and the only ones winning are the 1% hanging out safely in their gated communities or mansions!!!

It is absolutely vital for all of us to become smart and informed citizens who make decisions based on moral issues and not only financial gain. Become involved in politics which is nothing else but becoming involved in making decisions for our planet and the people that live on it.

Try to envision what people in other countries go through and experience because of us. Envision that drones from another countries fly over your home and drop a bomb on your babies in your yard. How would you feel?

Imagine your kids go to school and they never return because of another country dropping bombs on it. Imagine your mom is in the hospital and you get word that everybody in the hospital is dead including your mother because a foreign government that had no business being in your country bombed that hospital. How would you honestly feel?

That is what we have been doing to other countries!

We have to demand from our so called leaders or should we call them warmongers, to stop invading other countries and to start taking care of their people at home!

WTF Happened to Our Banks?

Well what happened is that Bill Clinton decided in 1999 to repeal the Glass-Steagall Act. Well what did Glass-Steagall actually do? The short of it is that commercial banking and investment banking had to be kept separate. In other words your money was safe in the bank no matter what the market would do and banks could not just merge indiscriminately with each other. After it was repealed the financial system and the bankers became very powerful and I noticed it myself.

I was banking with a certain bank and a year later they merged with another bank and another year later they merged again until within just a few years I was with bank number four, never having changed banks however. At the time I had no understanding what was going on.

The aftermath of that we could all feel during the financial crisis of 2007 and 2008. The investments became more and more risky and the banks that initially were more conservative also turned to riskier alternatives. The banks were basically playing poker with our money.

The outcome was disastrous for so many people and eventually the government bailed out the banks however regular people who lost their homes were not bailed out. Obama said we had to bail Wall Street out because they were too big to let them fail. Well now eight years later the banks have gotten even bigger and nobody has broken them up. Bernie was lobbying heavily for re-installing Glass-Steagall during his campaign knowing that we have to break up the banks *right now*.

However the banks of course have their own set of very powerful lobbyists and my worry is that our banking system will again fail and siphon of even more money from regular people. My belief is that the crisis of 2008 was merely a warm-up.

There is something however that you can do. Take your money out of the banks and put it into credit unions! Credit unions are independent from the banks and are beholden to the people. They are everywhere and you can easily do all your banking needs with them. So make the transfer and decide to no longer be part of this corrupt machine called the banking system!

WTF Happened to Student Loans?

Student loans, don't even get me started! How can a first world country not want to have the most educated populace possible? Studying should be free and how we pay for it is actually not that hard. We could siphon off a little bit of money from the war machine, which by the way takes half of our taxes, or we could charge Wall Street a fee for transactions.

We could simply decide as a nation to put money into areas that will benefit this country instead of destroying it. Every dollar spent on education comes back as seven dollars in the economy. It is an amazing return on our money if we invest in the future of our children!

Instead what has been done is that student loans are some of the higher loans in the country and at the same time there is no getting out of it, not even with bankruptcy anymore! It is a new form of slavery because young kids at the age of 20 to 22 years old already are so in debt that some of them could have bought a house from the money they spent on a four-year college degree. And a college degree at this point isn't worth anything anymore. My friend Sara when she graduated was the only one that had a full-time job lined up and it was not even in the field she studied it. It was at a doggy daycare but at least she had a full-time job unlike anybody else in her class!

State colleges and universities should be tuition free for everybody who has grades good enough to get in. All over Europe and most first world countries nobody has to pay for tuition. And yet this country, the richest country in the history of the world, kids come out of college with debt being anywhere from $30,000-$200,000.

In my eyes the solution is that students need to be in the streets demanding a drastic change! When they wanted to up the tuition in Canada by only $2000 per year, basically from $3000 up to $5000 a year the students were in the streets protesting every day until they tanked the idea. The same was true in Europe when they even hinted on the idea of starting to charge tuition. All the young people were in the streets and guess what happened, no tuition!!!

Of course banks and governments will not easily give up what they want to keep for themselves. Why would they not take all this money since we are so easily willing to give it to them? We have to wake up and demand better, we have to wake up and demand our taxes being used for good instead of evil, for tuitions instead of wars!

We have to get good at writing letters to congressmen as well as senators and to stand up for our rights, the alternative is that it will get worse for poor people and the middle class and the ultra wealthy will get more and more of the hard earned money of regular people! Income inequality is already staggering and it will not get better unless we stand up RIGHT NOW!!!

Doesn't it feel just like that to you?

Jill Stein (the Green Party president) has a wonderful idea, which is to bail out students. If she were to be president she would be able to appoint the chair of the Federal Reserve who in turn has the power to bail out students just like he had to power to bail out Wall Street. Of course this is the short and simple explanation and the long version would be more involved. But imagine a world where everybody who has student debt would be debt free. Instead young people would be able to buy a house or do other wonderful things with their money. Doesn't that sound so much better then paying off loans for education, which should have been free in the first place!

WTF Happened to Growing Food?

Hey 1%ers, what the fuck have you done to our food? All food used to be organic until about the 1950s. All of a sudden serious chemicals were used by farmers and the upside was that at first it felt like a lot more food was being produced, but in the long run we have realized that the soil is getting very poor and it is not a sustainable way of growing food, because pesticides and herbicides do not only attack one unwanted pests or weeds, they attack everything including the incredibly valuable microbes in our soil. But it was not enough to put the toxins on top of the plants; with the help of genetic engineering you are now able to put the toxins right inside the plants. Just from a commonsense standpoint you have to agree that this cannot be the right approach!

GMO's are dangerous because we simply do not have enough research on them to really make an educated decision on whether to use them or not. And by Monsanto having a revolving door at the FDA does not give me more confidence in this absolutely fucked up system. People that have worked for Monsanto end up working for the FDA then back to Monsanto and back again to the FDA. Like I said it is a revolving door that undermines the very core of what the FDA should be and stand for.

Have you guys noticed how many food choices we actually have? Did you notice there are only about three different types of potatoes, a couple different kinds of tomatoes, and everything has corn in it in one form or another, which of course is also GMO corn!

Our food diversity is totally in the shitter.

Now you might ask why does this matter and my answer is it matters an enormous amount because without diversity, if there is any sort of plight we are absolutely screwed. Diversity is what makes us less vulnerable. The Irish can tell you all about it with the potato famine in the 1800s. They used to have many different heirloom varieties of potatoes growing but then they found this one potato that was doing phenomenal in the Irish conditions. So everybody started growing that particular potato, well to make a long story short, blight attacked the potato and almost half the population of Ireland died. Diversity is our strength and we cannot let that die.

Grow some organic food!

Grow anything, grow a little herb plant on your windowsill if you live in an apartment or have planters on your balcony where you can grow tomatoes and cucumbers and different herbs. Everybody, truly everybody can grow some food. If you have a lawn transform it with the raised beds. If you have a flower garden add a few veggies in between. If you are planting trees make sure they are fruit or nut trees. There are so many creative ways to grow food even in apartments. You could have a hydroponic garden, which is not ideal in my eyes but still 1000 times better than store-bought produce.

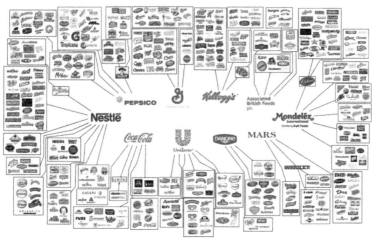

The illusion of choice

The solution is to reconnect with the earth and to look at what nature would do. Instead of fighting nature, work with it. It is less work and more reward!

Also make sure you get kids involved! Kids are our

future and they need to start loving the earth again. They intrinsically love playing with nature and we have to encourage them to do more of that every day. If you don't want your kids to grow up as crazy lunatics who are dangerous to society because of the brainwashing of video games and TV and the constant bombardment of violence, then you want to make sure that they learn to appreciate the planet and all its inhabitants, not just humans!

WHAT IF EVERY LAWN WAS TRANSFORMED INTO A FARM INSTEAD OF EXPENSIVE UPKEEP OF GRASS...
CHEF JOSE ANDRES

GROW FOOD, NOT LAWNS
DIY ▶ GARDENING ▶ LIVING ▶ NEWS ▶ MORE

WTF Happened to Our Food?

Hey corporate America, why is our food high in calories and low in nutrition nowadays? What does that mean in layman's terms? What that means is that most of our carbs come from white food. White rice, white bread, white pasta, and basically white empty shit! All the nutritious parts of a grain are in the shell and in the kernel, however that is all removed when it's being processed into white stuff. You do not want to eat that! You want to eat the *whole grain*!!! Whole grains are like a nice log on the fire that burns for a long time, unlike white grain, which is like straw, it's a burst of energy but it doesn't last.

So why is this shit even being sold to us? Well, part of the blame goes to us because we are lazy and we don't want to cook anymore so pre-packaged, pre-made, almost pre-chewed is easier but part of the blame goes to corporate America. The food manufacturers have learned that if they package crap into colorful boxes with beautiful labels they can sell us absolutely inferior food for a high price.

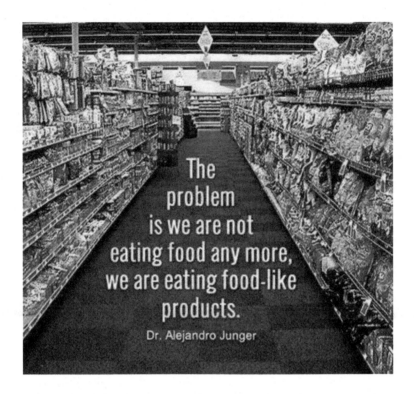

The problem is we are not eating food any more, we are eating food-like products.

Dr. Alejandro Junger

Our fruits and veggies are another thing altogether. They get hosed down with chemicals and people actually picking them have to wear masks and gloves because otherwise it would be too toxic. That alone should clue you in that it's not healthy to eat! On top of it, our produce will get irradiated to kill the enzymes in the food so they look pretty on the shelf for a long time, but are hard to digest. If that's not enough they will get coated with wax, of course to extend the shelf life of something that should have never been sold in the first place.

Our food at this point is highly processed and almost all of it contains corn or soy in one form or another. Read labels! There is hardly anything anymore that doesn't contain things like high fructose corn syrup or one if it's ugly cousins! Simply said that anything that is in a box you really don't want to eat. If you have to buy food at a regular grocery store because you don't have a farmers market or a co-op or a farm or a health food store nearby, make sure that you buy only on the outside perimeter of the store. Basically buy only in the produce section and if you are lucky they have an organic bakery with fresh baked goods.

Hey 99%ers what do you think we should do? As I mentioned above, we need to find alternative ways where we can get our food. There is just no two ways about it, if you actually want to stay or become healthy because the 1%ers certainly don't give a flying fuck about us, our health, or our future.

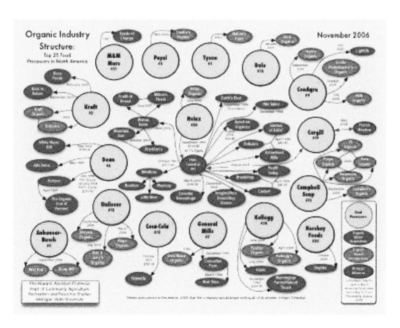

A lot of places have co-ops that are basically formed

by the citizens and owned by them, their prices are usually very good and they sell a lot of things in bulk. Also farmers markets are a vital part of a healthy food system. They give farmers the opportunity to sell directly to their customers and are cutting out the middleman, so often times that is also a way to save some money and get amazing food. CSA is an acronym for community supported agriculture where you basically give the farmer money at the beginning of the season and you will get produce all summer long that is fresh and amazingly delicious. All those options are of course a thorn in the eyes of corporate America and they are trying to slowly undermine those small businesses. They are passing laws in different states to make it harder for farms to sell directly to the public.

If you want to save this planet and your life you have to change your ways in a big way!

We seriously have to start cooking again. Cooking is not only healthy for the planet and ourselves in a physical way, but it also is a way to socialize and to build family relationships again that are desperately necessary in this country.

Imagine a world where your family is together in the kitchen and some people are chopping vegetables and others are kneading dough and somebody else is making cookies and everybody is telling stories and laughing, isn't that a much better vision than throwing a box in the microwave?

WTF Happened to Animal Agriculture?

I grew up on a little farm where we had a few cows, a couple pigs, and a bunch of chickens, geese, and ducks. They were kept pretty well although not perfect and when it was their time they would get slaughtered right on the farm except for the cows which we had for milk. The animals had it well because they were not only an investment and small farms could not afford to lose that investment, but they were also regarded as real beings that had feelings and emotions granted not to the point like humans in the eyes of farmers, but they understood that animals are alive. That is how most Farms looked 100 years ago or even still 60 years ago.

Boy has that changed!

Animals are no longer raised on farms; they are now raised in factories that have no regard for life. They are confined to spaces that are absolutely too small for even turning around, the food they get fed is no longer species correct food, cows get fed corn instead of grass which in turn creates E. coli bacteria which in turn makes humans sick. Where do you think mad cow disease came from! Cows who are absolute herbivores and never eat animal food were fed animal food! And we haven't learned a thing because now cows are the biggest ocean predators on the planet meaning they are eating more fish then anybody else! What the fuck!

In a little cage about the size of your iPad they hold

five or six chickens to lay eggs. As you can imagine the chickens go crazy! If you would be in a bathroom stall with six other people for two years you would also try to kill each other. So for the chickens not to be able to kill each other they cut the beaks off actually they burn them off and often times down to the nerve so they can no longer pick at each other. Humans have gone so far off the deep end for profits that it is completely wrong to call us humans because the word humanity is no longer a term that applies to us.

My friend Laura Aaron sent me this and I wanted to include it in this section because it is an incredibly valuable point:

Unless we challenge thousands of years of human domination by force, we ignore how we learned it in the first place and why violence is normalized in human society. "The entire civilization is "masculinized" since humans FIRST took license to dominate, subjugate, impregnate female animals as machines for animal agriculture, an obscene food production system that views female animals as products, property, commodities. Women AND men

80

beat that pathetic top of the food chain chest, that delusion that somehow it's a basic human right to confine, inseminate female animals and after they give birth to their own babies, abduct those babies to fatten, transport as juveniles, and slaughter. To understand human global conquer and dominate, oppress, subjugate the vulnerable for mass exploitation, we MUST understand the DNA that embeds in human society of the view of sentient animals as the underpinnings of the entire global economic machine... It's SO far back before Hillary became the warmonger and brute she has learned to become. It's SO far back our education system leaves it out because learning the foundation of masculine brute force, used in every corner of our dying planet, requires real education, not just manufactured assimilation into the herding culture. www.powerfulbook.com examines the path to the economic machine driven by conquer and exploit over cooperate and coexist... Interview Carol J Adams, author of The Sexual Politics of Meat, or Will Tuttle, author of The World Peace Diet, or Karen Davis, author of The Holocaust and Hen Maidens Tale...This is where the real and deeper answers reside for why human Patriarchal systems rise and fall on their own moral double edged sword, as the US is experiencing today. Hillary is a pawn in this system we ALL had a hand, and stomach in perpetuating. Ask any ethical vegan why domination and use of force has become a morally accepted norm. They get the foundation of this posture called SPECIESISM, the very first version of every other form of "ism" that sprung from it...

Eating animal food to the extent we do is killing people. There's so much science at this point that it creates most of our diseases. From cancer to heart attack to high cholesterol to hypertension they can all be traced back to eating too much protein. There is a wonderful video that you might want to consider watching. It is called Forks Over Knives and explains beautifully the connection between health and eating animals.

It is truly time to rethink what we put in our bodies and why. The Western world is addicted to food, mostly food that makes us sick, but not only ourselves it also makes our planet sick. Eating animals at the rate we do is killing our planet. Animal agriculture is the number one contributor to climate change! Yes I know I was thinking the same thing how could that be when we have all those CO_2 emissions from cars and planes. Well, all transportation combined only amounts to about 12 to 15% of greenhouse gas emissions. Animal agriculture in the most conservative of estimates amounts to 18% however some experts say it is as much as over 50%. There is a wonderful documentary called COWSPIRACY that you should definitely watch if you have any regard for our planet.

I myself have been a vegetarian/vegan for almost a couple decades with a few slips in between when I moved to Vermont. Vermont has a big farm to the table movement and a lot of animals here are raised the correct way. The problem is no animal wants to die and I realized that I can simply no longer be part of their suffering. We all have to rethink what we put into our bodies and I hope you will too! Not only will your own body be so grateful but you will be part of an ever-growing group of people that put kindness ahead of profits.

"The Idea that some lives matter less is the root of all that is wrong in this world"
Paul Farmer

NEVER LOSE YOUR SENSE OF OUTRAGE!

That is the reason I wrote this book!

There are so many other subjects that I am also outraged about but there is no book thick enough to write it all down.

Like Thomas Q. Williams pointed out, Obama is traveling around the country on taxpaper money to promote something we don't want and which will be devastating to us. WTF!

The Huffington Post complaining that nothing is being done about the election fraud and yet they endorsed Hillary. WTF!

That Native Americans got their whole country stolen and then after the white man committed genocide they are trying to destroy whatever is left. WTF!

That the 1/10,000 of 1% (as my friend Arthur Robbins pointed out) are so careless with our planet that you would think they can escape to another one once this one is completely unlivable for humans? WTF!

Why can't we simply use paper ballots to ensure every vote will be counted? WTF?

What if...!

We have the numbers, we have millions and when we truly recognize the strength we have we will have an amazing planet that will look very different from the one we have right now!

I would tell you to close your eyes and follow me on this journey of envisioning what it can look like if we all stand together but then you can't read ☺

What if there is a world where the color of our skin doesn't matter and we all have the same opportunities in life.

What if there is a world in which we honor and treat our Mother Earth the way Native Americans have done forever.

What if there is a world without war, where conflict is resolved peacefully and war is the very last resort if any.

What if there is a world where there is no hunger and all children have more then enough to eat and have the right to still be children, play, get out in nature and learn to respect and treat each other with kindness and love.

What if there is a world where every job is important and pays a living wage no matter what it is.

What if there is a world where mothers or fathers can stay with their children until they are at the age of going to school.

What if there is a world where success is measured in smiles and happiness.

What if there is a planet where LOVE is our guiding light not fear…

What if…

" I beg of you, do not enter this world of despair, we can win this fight if we stand together"

- Bernie Sanders 2015 -

CPSIA information can be obtained at www.ICGtesting.com
Printed in the USA
BVOW05s1137280816

460125BV00009BA/9/P